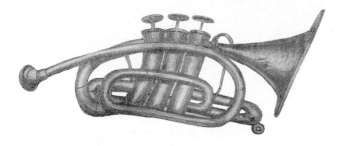

And here, here was a real, live jazz band in all its pulsing beauty. He was dying to watch the musicians, to see how they held their instruments, to study how they stood, just to lay eyes on them.

Louis dropped to his knees, and his ebony eyes followed the feet of the oh-so-slow dancers. Crouching, all he could see were dancing feet!

PLAY, LOUIS, PLAY!

The True Story of a
Boy and His Horn

Muriel Harris Weinstein
ILLUSTRATED BY Frank Morrison

BLOOMSBURY
NEW YORK   LONDON   NEW DELHI   SYDNEY

First published in the United States of America in December 2010
by Bloomsbury Children's Books
Paperback edition published in January 2013
www.bloomsburykids.com

For information about permission to reproduce selections from this book, write to
Permissions, Bloomsbury Children's Books, 175 Fifth Avenue, New York, New York 10010

The Library of Congress has cataloged the hardcover edition as follows:
Weinstein, Muriel Harris.
Play, Louis, play! : the true story of a boy and his horn / Muriel Harris Weinstein ;
illustrated by Frank Morrison.
p.   cm.
ISBN 978-1-59990-375-0 (hardcover)
1. Armstrong, Louis, 1901–1971—Juvenile literature. 2. Jazz musicians—United States—
Biography—Juvenile literature. 3. African American jazz musicians—Juvenile literature.
I. Morrison, Frank, ill. II. Title.
ML3930.A75W45 2011   781.65092—dc22   [B]   2010025974

ISBN 978-1-59990-994-3 (paperback)

Art created with pencil
Book design by Donna Mark
Typeset by Westchester Book Composition

Printed in the U.S.A. by Thomson-Shore, Dexter, Michigan
2 4 6 8 10 9 7 5 3 1

Manufactured by Thomson-Shore, Dexter, MI (USA); RMA586LS776, November, 2012

To my grandchildren,
Leah, Hannah,
Samuel, Ian, Aidan, and Riley

The horn was an extension of Louis
Louis' voice was his horn
Louis and his horn were one

And this is their story.

PLAY, LOUIS, PLAY!

CHAPTER 1

How Did Louis Discover Music?

There isn't a jazzman in New Orleans who hasn't tapped my brain about Louis Armstrong. They talk to me as if sugar's sprinkled on their tongue. "Hey, you knew Louis like no one else. What's the pitch, the real story?"

These jazzmen know *I know*. I ought to. I was Little Louis' horn, the first horn he ever played. He'd talk to me as if we were brothers, tell me every note in his life. Words poured out like soda pop.

The first time I saw Louis I was in a run-down, dusty hock-shop window on Perdido, the muddiest street in New Orleans. My body was dented, my life slowly tarnishing away, when I noticed this raggle-taggle kid looking in the window. He showed up each and every morn when the sun cracked open. I bet he was about six years at most, so skinny you knew nothing was sliding into his belly. And there was nothing on his feet. No matter how muddy the streets were, he was barefoot. Well, he'd stop and eye me through the window and sigh. His sigh held so much wanting, I could feel it through the glass.

Louis liked to pretend that he had a horn and, with his lips curling out, he'd

hum and blow as if he were playing a cornet.

When kids passed by they'd yell, "Whatcha doin'? You look like a fish face."

But Louis never sang a sour note. His answer danced the two-step right out of his mouth. "I'm practicin'. Can't ya *hear* it?"

The kids laughed, specially Little Louis.

Louis' smile traveled from one side of his face clear over to the other. Everyone said it was as wide as an open satchel. So they called him "Satchelmouth." The nickname stuck. And it wasn't until later that Satchelmouth was shortened to Satchmo.

He also answered to Little Louis, Dippermouth, and Gatemouth. There were always kids who said, "Hey, that's a put-down name. Ya won't catch me usin' it."

Louis would laugh and say, "A good nickname's hard to find. And I'm aimin' to keep all of them." Yeah, he was a cool cat.

Louis lived with his grandma because his momma, Mayann, worked cleaning houses and sometimes had to sleep over. Louis' dad, a worker in a turpentine factory, had left the family when Louis was born. Grandma and Louis lived on Jane Alley in the Back O' Town, the toughest section in New Orleans. It was so tough everyone called it the Battlefield.

To make a living, Grandma took in washing and ironing. Louis helped by carrying the washboard, handing her clothespins for the clothesline, and sometimes folding pillowcases with her.

Louis couldn't wait for Sundays. That

day shone as if the sun were wrapped inside it. He'd awake at the crack of dawn and start rushing his grandma to get to church on time. "Church singin' fills me up better than breakfast," he'd say. He didn't want to miss a single hymn. The singing and clapping rhythm crawled into his little body and jiggled around there for the rest of the week. Louis was discovering music, and it became his favorite food, his favorite way of spending time.

CHAPTER 2

Can a Kid, a Young Kid, Rescue His Family?

When Louis told me about his life, complaints never fell from his tongue. He said they hurt his ears as much as a horn's sour notes. Louis said he was about six when he had to leave his grandma. His momma, Mayann, was sick and couldn't work. She had had another baby, his little sister, Beatrice. His dad had gone back to Mayann for a few months, but that old freedom itch crawled into his shoes again. That man just couldn't stay put. And like before, he ran so fast through the back door you'd think a skunk was chasing him. So Louis had to go home and take care of his momma and Beatrice.

Beatrice probably caught what her momma had, and together they were weaker than weeds in a hurricane.

So Mayann sent a note to Grandma that was full of the blues. Mayann said she needed Little Louis' help. It didn't matter how young he was, she just needed him.

Louis hadn't seen his momma in a l-o-n-g time. Neither Grandma nor Mayann had cars, so they couldn't visit each other. And they didn't have enough coins jingling in their pockets for the trolley car.

It wasn't easy leaving Grandma. Louis loved her. She packed his two pairs of hand-me-down pants, ten sizes too big; sewed the holes in his two hand-me-down shirts; and put them in a paper bag. Then she dressed him in his white, Sunday "goin' to church" suit with the fancy ruffled collar.

Grandma said if she hugged him, she might never let him go. Instead, she stood at her front door, waving good-bye. Louis stood at the fence gate, biting his lips to keep from crying.

That moment really stuck with Louis. He told me that story over and over, like a chorus in a song. And I know that his heart cracked like a branch on an old swamp tree when he left. Lucky thing Louis had a knack for looking at the bright side. That's part of what made him special.

. . .

Mayann had two tiny rooms without electricity or running water. And if that weren't bad enough, she had no inside toilets—only outside toilets called outhouses. They were lined up in the backyard, one row for men and one row for women.

The sight of his momma lying sick in bed upset Louis so much that he didn't give a hoot about inside toilets or outside toilets or even running water. He rushed to her and sat on the edge of her bed. "Momma, I helped Grandma," he said. "And now I can help you. Help you get better. Tell me what to do and *boom*, it'll be done."

Mayann's face lit up. "My, you *are* one fine son," she said. Then she asked him if he was strong enough to pick up one of the loose floorboards for her purse. Mayann explained that under the floorboard was a hiding place. She had to keep her things safe there because some people in the neighborhood stole to help pay the rent and buy food. It wasn't easy making a living.

She asked Louis to take fifty cents out of her purse and walk all the way to Rampart Street to get her medicine. It was the first time someone trusted him with such a big errand. Louis felt real grown-up.

Walking to the drugstore was an ear-popping treat. Dance halls, bars, and honky-tonks lined the streets and music flowed out: the blues, ragtime, jazz. Louis' ears flapped with joy. A street band jazzing up "Maple Street Rag" passed by. Louis knew they had just returned from a funeral. New Orleans bands played mournful music on the way to the grave, but after the ceremony they jazzed away with *oobalie doo dop*. They'd swing so high, it made you wanna dance.

Grandma always said, "Life goes on after someone passes, so people must think of good things. And music sure is one of them."

Mayann's neighborhood was as rough as the Battlefield. But Little Louis never noticed that. Music was all he heard: horns *wah-wah-wah*ing, slow 'n' sad drag-me-out blues, riffs on razzmatazz cornets, and jazzy beats of thumping piano keys. Their sounds, like waves in an ocean, rolled into him, flooded his ears, and flowed through his body.

There were so many of the little dance

halls called honky-tonks, it was hard to find the drugstore. His eyes finally spotted it, a tiny place. He paid fifty cents for Mayann's herbal syrup, and again that grown-up feeling returned. Clutching the medicine, Louis raced home with such speed his feet scorched the streets.

"Child, you sure have fast feet," Mayann said as Louis walked in. "You are one big blessing."

He gave Mayann the syrup, and she started feeling better in no time.

Then he wanted to feed baby Beatrice, nicknamed Mama Lucy, but the cupboards were bare. There was nothing to eat. Louis finally found an old, half-full box of dried beans. Luckily, Mayann had a large pot of rainwater on the windowsill. He mixed it with the red beans and they cooked. Mama Lucy licked her lips.

So did Mayann—and before you could say "Come blow your horn," his sister and momma were in dreamland.

When Louis heard Mayann snoring, he hightailed it outside. His ears ached to hear that music again.

As Louis walked, his mind ragged him. Worries scurried through his head. He asked himself, *How can I help Mayann? There's no food. Tonight there were some red beans, but not another thing! And the beans were old, dried up.* They needed to eat. He thought, *So what if I'm a kid? I can help out. I can make money. But how?*

Then Louis heard the bands practicing. His worries drifted off like notes floating out of a horn. With the music in his ears, he leaped over muddy puddles, bare feet flying as fast as fingers on a hot trumpet. Louis thought that music was the best thing anyone could have. There was nothing better in heaven or on earth.

Louis was in luck! As he came up to Pete Lala's place, a dance club, he spotted a broken board in the wall, hanging down real loose so there was a big gap. Louis couldn't believe it. All his life music had surrounded him, filled him—but except for the marching bands, his eyes had never seen a jazz group. And here, here was a real, live jazz band in all its pulsing beauty. He was dying to watch the musicians, to see how they held their instruments, to study how they stood, just to lay eyes on them.

Louis dropped to his knees, and his ebony eyes followed the feet of the oh-so-slow dancers. Crouching, all he could see were dancing feet!

Louis looked to the right and to the left, making sure nobody would catch him. Then he bent over and slowly crawled through the gap. Good thing he was so small.

Inside was dark and smoky. There was a table nearby. Louis hid under it. His eyeballs glued themselves to the band.

The musicians! Louis thought they had to be the Lord's happiest men. How did they blow with such beauty? The cornets talked to him. He knew he *had* to

play one. He was so caught up in the sound that when a fight broke out by the front door, Louis never heard the ruckus. This music, the music the colored musicians made, was like wings carrying him to heaven.

CHAPTER 3

Can Little Louis Make Money?

That Little Louis' mind was always racing. Every day he'd come up with a new idea for making a buck. I still remember one spring morning when I was enjoying the sun splashing through my hock-shop window. And who do I see but Little Louis, who was about seven now, sitting on top of a horse-drawn cart with one of the Karnofsky boys. The cart was filled with rags, bones, bottles, metal and iron scraps. They rattled and peddled up and down the New Orleans streets, trading and selling. Little Louis blew a toy horn with such force, he sounded like an army bugler. That toy horn blared, "C'mon out, everybody! Lookit what we've got! You won't be sorry!"

Everyone knew the Karnofsky cart, and the minute it showed up there was a crowd waiting. The Karnofskys were a family of Russian Jews who lived on the edge of the colored section. Little Louis was like a member of their family. At night, old lady Karnofsky refused to send him home until she filled his belly with good Jewish food.

Their evenings always ended in song. Mrs. Karnofsky, holding little David in her arms, sang "The Russian Lullaby."

It became Louis' favorite. He joined in, and the memories of singing with them nested in his heart.

"First you eat. Then you go to your momma," she said each time. When the Karnofsky kids gave him a Star of David necklace, Louis said it would hang on his neck forever.

Then I remember another morning, about a year later, when I looked out my window to see this kid standing on my corner, shouting, "EXTRA! EXTRA! READ ALL ABOUT IT! GET YER PAPER, MISTER!"

I knew the voice. It was Little Louis. He'd convinced White Charlie, the guy in charge of the paper route, that he could sell more papers than any other kid. White Charlie liked him. Said Louis had spunk. He was about eight or nine then and—get this—still working on the Karnofsky cart, blowing his toy horn. He was one little hustler.

Around this time, Mayann said Louis had to go to school. The Fisk School for Boys had no money, no library, no textbooks, no supplies of any kind to help the students. Sometimes five or six students had to share one book, and its pages were often ripped or missing. That's because the school was segregated and the government never gave the same amount of money for supplies to colored schools as they did to white schools. So the colored kids didn't receive enough books and, worse, the books they did have were old or outdated. Some of their teachers weren't even teachers. They either had no training or were inexperienced.

Still, Louis wanted to go to school. He

wanted to learn. But it didn't last long. He had so much worry about how to support Mayann and Mama Lucy that making money for food and rent was the only thought running around in his head. And since he didn't have books to take home and study, Louis dropped out. He was in fifth grade then.

Would you believe that when the sun opened its eye the next morning, Louis was on the corner singing in a quartet? There was Big Nose Sydney, Little Mack, Happy Bolton, and Little Louis. They sang in perfect four-part harmony, each boy singing different notes. That's no easy-breezy thing to do. Their ears were as sharp as razors.

Little Louis heard such wonderful harmony and melodies in his head that he *improvised*—that is, he made up other

notes on the spot to sing along with the melody. Sometimes he even said to heck with the words and his voice flew, as free as a bird, soaring and dipping with sounds like *beedle reee-eep, ooblee-ooo-dooo*, and *jippity jin joon*. That was *scat*, a tricky-slicky thing to do.

Was that quartet a hit! They sang at the docks and on every street corner. Everyone loved them. The boys passed their hats and those hats overflowed. As soon as they divvied up the money, Louis made a beeline for his house and dropped his share smack into Mayann's lap.

People on Perdido and Rampart streets loved Little Louis as if he were their son. Louis, full of smiles, always said hello and asked about their family or their sick uncle or their sore throat. They said he cared. He wasn't putting on an act. And when his quartet sang, they'd come out and listen.

Little Louis needed money so bad that he thought up things no one else did. Did he have imagination! He tried to make money through music, so he made a "gut-box," an instrument built from a cigar box with four wires down its body. He played that gut-box while he was singing in the groups. Its twangy sound tickled his ears.

Louis also read the daily paper to the Old Folks. Whenever Mayann complained he wasn't in school, he said that he was reading more now by reading to the Old Folks, and it was better than school 'cause he was learning hard words. And he'd add, "Momma, my mind's learnin' so much 'bout the world. If my teachers heard me read they'd be clappin' and doin' handstands."

Louis had so little money he could only buy the two cheapest things to eat: fish heads and beans. Sometimes he didn't have money even for that. But Little Louis never sang a sour note about it.

One afternoon Little Louis walked to the fruit store. I could see him. You see, I lived in the hock-shop window, right across the street, opposite the fruit store. And there, in front of the store, was a big basket bulging with fat bananas. They were so yellow they looked painted. Boy, did they tempt Louis. There were so many that Louis must've figured a banana or two wouldn't be missed. Before you could blow a note, Louis' hand jumped out and grabbed a small bunch—just a few. He quickly put them inside his shirt. But a policeman was watching. He blew his whistle and shouted, "Thief, STOP!"

Louis didn't know which way to go, left, right, or straight ahead. A second cop heard the whistle and came running. With a cop on each side, there was no place for Louis to run except into a puddle of mud. They caught him, slapped handcuffs on him, and pulled him to their station. I had a front-row seat from my window.

Don't ask how I felt. I wanted to tell the cops what a good kid he was, how hard he was trying to make money, how hungry he was. But I was imprisoned in that window, my glass cage, waiting for

Louis to get enough money so he could set me free and blow his wonderful music.

Louis told the police that it was only food, that his family needed to eat. He said he wasn't stealing anything serious, like diamonds or gold. But they booked him—they wrote his name down in a file. They also made sure he knew that *stealing was stealing*, no matter what!

The police let him go with the promise that he'd never do it again. The trouble was that, as much as Louis added to Mayann's budget, the money was never enough to feed them. And it sure wasn't enough to buy a horn, his Big Dream.

CHAPTER 4

Why Did Louis Give Up His Horn Money?

Mayann felt lucky she had Louis. While she never had enough food for him, she did feed him praise. She told him he was smart and full of good plans for making money. Then she reminded him that getting ahead meant work, work, and more work. Nothing was free.

One afternoon Louis made so much money that he came home with coins in

his pockets jingling like a Christmas bell. And his paper bag bulged with money— a fortune! He told Mayann that finally, finally he could buy his horn.

"Louis," she said, "don't you know today's your sister's birthday? And my old eyes tell me you have just enough money for Mama Lucy's birthday supper. Now we can make her favorite dish, jambalaya."

"Awww, May-ann!" Louis sighed.

Usually he was the first one to give money or share it. Now he shifted from foot to foot. He felt he'd die if he didn't get his horn. But he thought about it for a few more beats, and the music that flowed out of his mouth was, "Sure 'nuff, Mayann. Celebrating Mama Lucy's birthday is what we've got to do. Here, take the money."

Louis' heart cracked like an old clamshell. But he always liked making others happy, and he knew he'd feel *worse* if he turned Mayann down. His supper would never slide down his gullet if he nixed Mama Lucy's birthday celebration. So he told himself, *I'll just wait a little bit longer.* Then he broke into a big smile and hugged his momma.

That night Little Louis couldn't spoon enough jambalaya into his big mouth. He

said it was the best jambalaya Mayann ever cooked up. He licked his chops all the way into dreamland.

• • •

Sometimes when Mayann had to clean a house a long distance away, she slept over there. And when Mayann slept over, she never allowed Louis and Mama Lucy to stay alone in the apartment.

Mayann would call her brother, Ike Miles, and he'd come and get Louis and Mama Lucy. Louis and Mama Lucy were crazy about going to Uncle Ike's. He had eight children, and when all ten kids got together, it was a happy ruckus. They'd bounce and jump, scramble around, roll over each other, and leap from bed to floor and from floor to bed again. There were so many of them on the bed that they sometimes fell off—and then they'd plop onto a floor mattress and fall asleep right there. Louis and Mama Lucy knew Mayann would never like the shenanigans going on.

Sometimes Ike had to go back to the factory to work, and since he didn't have a wife, the kids were all alone. Usually it was no problem—Louis would make supper and everybody helped clean up. But one night all ten of them were up the whole night, all twelve hours, rolling and bouncing on each other on the bed and on the floor. When morning came, Louis and Mama Lucy had sleep in their eyes and they couldn't stop yawning. They couldn't even lift their eyelids open. Their feet just shuffled along.

Mayann was as mad as water boiling in a kettle. "Listen here!" she screamed.

"You two can't go to Uncle Ike's ever again . . . no more! Not until Uncle Ike gets himself a wife."

Little Louis and Mama Lucy just smiled at each other because they knew it wouldn't be long. Uncle Ike was always on the lookout for a wife.

CHAPTER 5

Then How Did Little Louis Get His Horn?

Every horn loves a parade. Lucky for me, no city had more parades than New Orleans. There was a parade every day, marching right past my window. And if there was a funeral, there might be more than one! There wasn't a person in all of New Orleans, rich or poor, who wanted to die without a band at their funeral.

I remember the day they buried old

lady Fanton. On the way to the funeral, the horns moaned so low they sounded like weeping women. But the minute the body was lowered into the grave, the band struck up one of those good old tunes, "When the Saints Go Marching In," and everyone left their worries behind. The music talked to their feet and their feet talked to the sidewalk. The spirit hit them as they sang and marched.

When they marched into town, the music was so lively even the stores emptied. The band strutted and blew their horns, swaying from side to side. The brass horns, as bright as the sun, were mellow and full of honey. The drum hung from a wide ribbon around the drummer's neck, and the big tuba tooted away. The players all marched in such a snappy rhythm that you forgot who they had buried and could think nothing but *My feet wanna dance.*

Louis jumped into the second line of the funeral parade and made believe he was blowing a cornet. His feet stepped so lively, they burned the cement.

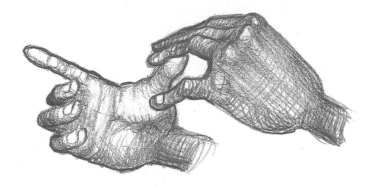

That night when Louis got to the Karnofskys', he couldn't wait to tell them about the parade. And when he told how he made believe he blew a horn, Mrs. Karnofsky said that the music inside him was a gift. Mr. Karnofsky said that music had to be in his life. Their caring made Little Louis feel special.

The following day, Louis and Alexander, one of the Karnofsky boys, went out in the cart to peddle old clothes and metal. Louis, as usual, blew on the toy horn. Only this time, he had taken off the tin piece at the top of the horn, and now he put his two fingers there instead. It worked! He blew so loud and clear that all the shopkeepers ran outside. Alexander applauded. "I can't believe the tone you get out of that toy horn. If I weren't sitting here, I'd bet it was a real horn."

Louis felt good. But what happened next made him feel even better. Alexander pulled two bucks and a fifty-cent piece from his hip pocket. Then Alexander said, "I don't want you to waste your talent. Here, take this. It's a loan. It'll help you get your cornet faster."

Wow! I couldn't believe it. It was for me, the five-dollar horn in the hock-shop window.

Tears spilled out of Little Louis' eyes. His hands shook like a pair of maracas as he held the money. "I'll save fifty cents a week. Just watch me. In five weeks, just five weeks, I'll have enough to buy the horn. Then I'll pay you back. I promise."

In five weeks, true to his word, Louis' savings added up to two bucks and fifty cents. He added Alexander's two-fifty loan and raced to the hock shop, singing, "I'm gonna hold that horn to my lips, *ooblee-loon-lee*. I'm gonna blow that horn as I skip, *ooblee-boom-bee*."

Louis danced into the hock shop. But he skidded to a stop. There was another kid—and the kid was holding *me*, Louis' horn!

Oh no! Louis thought. *He* can't *buy it.*

I've been saving a long time. That horn 'n' me, we belong to each other.

Louis stood back a minute, watching, thinking. For a split second, he thought of butting in, telling the owner, "That horn's been waitin' for me . . . it's MINE!" But Louis had a fair streak as wide as the Mississippi. With a broken heart, he told himself, *If that kid came first, then he gets it. That's the way life is.*

The kid was holding me, holding me up to the light. And me, well, I was near to turning blue from holding my breath. Never did I want to go with that kid.

That's when the kid saw the dent in my side. He put me down so quickly you'd think I had a disease! He told the pawn-broker, "This horn's no good. I thought it was in better condition. Forget it!" And he was out the door.

Louis wanted to jump through the roof. Everything inside him jiggled with joy. This proved that the horn was his . . . only his.

And what a relief for me!

Louis soft-shoed up to the counter. He put the five bucks down. When Louis picked me up, I wanted to blow so darn loud that all the horn players in New Orleans would cry, "Now, *that's* what I call a horn."

Louis looked at my old, stained body and said he could shine me up so good I'd make everyone squint. Then—without ever reading a note, without ever taking a lesson—Little Louis picked me up, puckered his lips, and blew "Home, Sweet Home" as if it were born on his tongue.

The owner, his helper, and a few people outside the store stopped what

they were doing and just listened. A crowd gathered, as if it were a concert. The sound of that horn was like molasses pouring out, thick and sweet. The owner said, "That Little Louis, he must've come into this world blowing a horn."

CHAPTER 6

Why Was Louis Carrying a Gun?

Little Louis never went anywhere without me, his horn. Every night I went with him to the honky-tonks to hear the great Joe Oliver. Louis admired him more than any other horn man. Joe Oliver played the cornet. And Louis wanted to play like him. Oliver played with Kid Ory and Bunk Johnson. Louis loved to listen to the cornets and trumpets sing out.

Louis had a special gift—he could hear music only once and his brain recorded it note for note. He could play it back in his mind any time, even years later. How many musicians could do that? And how he blew! Long, sweet notes poured out, trembling in the air like honeysuckle on a vine, lingering in your ear long after he blew them.

Well, time flew like a good horn solo. It was 1913. Little Louis was about eleven now. He felt grown-up and couldn't believe that New Year's Eve had arrived. All the kids loved that holiday because New Orleans was like a merry-go-round filled with music, fireworks, torches, and Roman candles. Some guys loved noise so much that they brought guns. Of course, the bullets were blank. The police didn't like them, but they weren't against the law.

Just a few days before, Louis had seen his mother's boyfriend hide a gun in the bottom drawer of the dresser. So on New Year's Eve, without asking his mother, Louis took the gun when he left the apartment. It was the first time he ever held one. He hid it in his hip pocket.

As he walked, Little Louis felt strange. He really wasn't comfortable with the gun. It was as if the gun didn't belong in his pocket. But instead of putting it back, he kept it and patted his pocket, protecting it there.

Well, on this day Louis' quartet was singing on Perdido Street. Suddenly a guy on the opposite side of the street pulled a six-shooter from his pocket and fired a blank straight in Little Louis' direction. So Big Nose Sydney said, "C'mon Louis, go get 'im."

Louis pulled out the gun and shot it straight up in the air. Even though the gun held blanks, it sounded exactly like real bullets, and the kid who had started it leaped into some alley faster than a grace note.

Everyone ran for cover but Little Louis. He stood there, frozen, alone. The noise shocked him.

The cops came running. "You're under arrest, kid," the big cop said, "for shooting bullets."

"They were blanks," Louis said. "I didn't hurt no one. Please, please don't arrest me. You gotta let me go home to my momma. She'll worry."

The police refused to let him go. In those days the police had a lot of power

and the colored people had none, and the police were often mean, even if it was a kid they were arresting. They had also picked up Louis before, for stealing food. So they pushed him into the paddy wagon.

Hunched over in a dark corner, all the way in the back, Louis' body couldn't stop trembling. He buried his fists in his eyes to stop the flood of tears. But his fists couldn't hold them back. His shirt got so wet you'd think he was just baptized. Fear shook his body. Even his hands and legs were shaking. The police were taking him away, and he didn't know when he'd come back.

CHAPTER 7

How Did a Bad Thing
Turn into a Good Thing?

All his life, Louis had heard terrible stories about the Colored Waif's Home for Boys. And now he was going there. Not only was he alone but, worse, he was without me . . . me, his horn. And how do you think I felt when I heard Louis would be taken away?

The Colored Waif's Home was out in the country, way out. The horses clopped on the gravel path in an easy rhythm. They knew the road blindfolded, but Louis told me later that he hoped they'd lose their way.

When the wagon finally stopped and Louis jumped out, he couldn't believe his eyes. There were acres and acres of grassy land. Huge trees spread their arms out as if to hug the Lord. Gardens surrounded the building; green was the only color he could see. Across the road was the biggest dairy farm around, where hundreds of cows, bulls, calves, and some horses lived. What a difference between this and the muddy streets and run-down shacks of the Battlefield.

Louis kept sniffing. "What's *that*?" he asked.

"Honeysuckle, child," was the answer.

"That smell's gotta come from heaven,"

Louis said. His nose sniffed the air like a bird dog's. He had never smelled anything so good.

The Home was a combination orphanage and reform school. It was an old building—but, oh, so clean. The boys there scoured and scrubbed and polished it till it shone. Louis had to wash the dishes, dry the dishes, scrub the floor, paint, and clean the toilets. Those boys dusted and polished every shelf, every table, every piece of furniture in that Home. Louis didn't mind the hard work. He did everything expected of him; he even enjoyed it. Would you believe they also raised their fruits and vegetables in gardens surrounding the building? Yes sirree, they grew the food they ate.

Louis settled into a ward of twelve or fifteen boys. Every morning a big warm breakfast was on his table and every night clean sheets were on his bed. Louis couldn't believe it. He had never had this before.

Now, everyone knew how Louis' tongue loved to wag. Every thought in his head wiggled right down to his tongue. In the Home, without a special friend like me to listen to his thoughts, Louis discovered that he liked writing about his life on pads or in notebooks. That was the beginning of Louis' journals. He loved to write—words and music.

His mile-long smile and friendly ways won the hearts of the kids and the staff . . . except for Mr. Davis, the director of the band. He said any kid from the Battlefield was not to be trusted. He said Louis was trouble.

Every day, without missing a beat,

Louis hung around Mr. Davis's band, his singing heart aching to join them. He loved listening to their rehearsals—and they rehearsed every single day, rain or shine. One morning Mr. Davis thought, *This kid's sticking to me like a fly to fly-paper. Maybe he's really interested.* So he asked Louis to try out.

Little Louis jumped out of his skin. "Yessssssirrr. I'm dyin' to try."

Louis expected a horn. Mr. Davis gave him a tambourine. Another kid would've turned down the tambourine. Not Little Louis. He shook that tambourine with such a bouncy rhythm that angels above wiggled their hips.

Then Mr. Davis offered him the drums.

Though Louis was still aching for a horn, he just smiled, took the drum, and slapped his fingers against its tight canvas skin as if they were drumsticks. Mr. Davis was impressed. When Louis sang along or hummed and drummed, he heard Louis' perfect pitch and perfect timing. So he finally offered Louis a horn.

Louis was so happy, he danced everywhere. He just plain forgot how to walk.

How could he not like it there? He had his music morning, noon, 'n' night. For the first time in his life, he never worried about his next meal. For the first time, he wore shoes and had clean clothes and his very own bed.

Yet down down deep he longed for home, for his momma, for Mayann. True, she visited him weekly, but he still missed living with her. His dream was going back to his family and to his New Orleans, the city that talked to him, the city that sang to him.

Mr. Davis's band marched every week. They marched into all sections of New Orleans. And when they were to march into Louis' old neighborhood, all the neighbors, all his friends, and even the musicians that played in honky-tonks took time off to see *their* Louis. They ran to Mayann shouting, "Louis is coming! Louis is coming!"

The entire neighborhood turned out for the Colored Waif's Home Band. They never expected to see Little Louis leading the band. But there he was. He strutted down the streets as if he were a five-star conductor and blew his horn with such a swinging tempo that all the honky-tonk

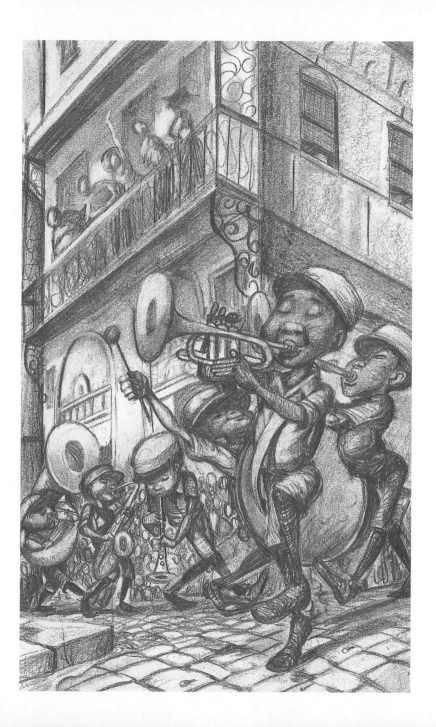

cornetists cried, "Holy moly, I better practice!"

Joy bubbled in Louis' heart when he saw his town welcome him. He never expected this. People lined the streets as if he were a hero. Instead of the usual candy that people threw at parades, his neighbors and friends took up a collection of money just for their Louis. Coins and bills overflowed every hat that was passed. Mr. Davis's eyes bulged when he saw how the town loved Little Louis. He counted the money twice. There was such a pile of coins and bills that Mr. Davis bought the band new instruments *and* new uniforms.

Time passed as fast as a bee buzzing from one flower to another. Louis was in the Colored Waif's Home for six months, twelve months, and before you knew it, it was a year 'n' a half. His behavior was so good, Louis was allowed to leave. But Mayann didn't make enough money to support Louis. The head of the Home said that if she wanted Louis back, she needed to make more money. Louis was stuck like a fly in a glue pot.

CHAPTER 8

How Did Louis Get Out of the Colored Waif's Home?

Louis' father, Willie, never gave two hoots for him. But one day, when Louis was about fourteen, Willie went to the Home to get him. His father said that he and his wife would be happy to support Louis. What Willie did *not* say was that he needed Louis to care for his two young sons. His dad had finally settled down, remarried, and had two other kids.

Since Willie and his wife both worked, they needed Louis.

Louis was not in tune with his dad's idea. He would rather have stayed at the Home, playing his music and practicing with the band. He didn't know his father. It was like going with a stranger.

But like I said before, Louis didn't sing any sour notes. He smiled and said he'd do his best. And he meant it.

Louis cooked, cleaned, and scrubbed the apartment while caring for his half brothers. Those two were like a pair of prizefighters, not happy unless they were fighting.

He had no time to play his music or even listen to it. But he had made a promise and Mayann always said, "A promise is a promise. You gotta keep it."

One day his father told Louis that

Gertrude, his wife, would be having another baby. And without even a word of thanks, without the sound of caring in his voice, he said, "With the new baby coming any day, there'll be no money for extra food. So, Louis, you'll have to leave."

Louis' father didn't care where he went. He said he could go anywhere, even back to Mayann's. When Louis heard that, his smile lit up like a three-hundred-watt bulb. He ran faster than a rabbit running from a hunter. He was free again! He could play his horn. He could sing. He could listen to his music. And he'd see Mayann, his wonderful momma. He was so excited that he raced all the way to Mayann's place.

When Louis walked in, you'd think it was the Fourth of July. Mama Lucy and Mayann kept laughing and hugging and kissing him. They were all so happy to see one another that their lips couldn't stop curling into smiles.

Mayann made Louis' favorite dish, jambalaya, and Louis took me, his horn, off the shelf, dusted me off, and told the family how much he missed me. Then he played and played far into the night. And what do you think he played first? "Home, Sweet Home."

CHAPTER 9

Razzle-Dazzle, He's Home. But How Does He Make a Buck?

Was it good to have Louis home again! He blew notes so sweet, the other horns turned green. And after Louis played "Home, Sweet Home," he told me he could make me shine like a new horn.

"You'll look as golden as homemade butter," Louis said. His hands cleaned and rubbed, polishing till his fingers hurt. I was so bright he didn't need a light in the room.

Next thing you know, Louis got a job playing cornet in Pete Lala's band at Henry Ponce's place, one of the bigger honky-tonks. He played cornet all night. At four, he'd drag himself home and grab some sleep, about two or three hours' worth. Then he'd shovel coal from seven in the morning till five in the afternoon.

Then he'd hightail it to his quartet to sing.

He brought home a big seventy-five

cents a day for shoveling coal. He was thankful for that money. Louis' quartet was the best, but by the time they divvied up their earnings there wasn't much left, and each singer filled his pockets with pennies. And I do mean pennies. But Louis loved singing so much that he didn't give a darn. He was just glad music was in his life again.

At the Home they had played only marches. Louis loved the marches, but there was more to music than marches. So coming home was like feeding his starving soul.

But life was not all honey 'n' flapjacks. At the end of each day Louis' back would kill him. It was crying out for some rest. He knew the pain was from shoveling coal. He purposely didn't tell Mayann about it, because then she'd make him quit one of the jobs. How could he quit Pete Lala's band? Playing his horn at Henry Ponce's was being in heaven. He was playing *his* music—the blues, jazz, ragtime—and playing it with musicians he admired. He felt alive playing.

And how could he quit the coal job? That gave him dough, money, greenbacks . . . for *real food.* And quit the quartet? Never! Out of the question. So he ignored the pain. Louis struggled on with little money and a bad back—but, oh, what a joyful spirit!

The summer that Louis turned eighteen, he thought he'd try playing his horn on one of the riverboats paddling up and down the Mississippi. They welcomed Louis with open arms. Fate Marable, the leader of the band, was sure their customers would double once the people

heard Louis play. Fate was right. Louis was so good, folks stood on the docks waiting for his boat to pass. They wanted to hear the haunting sound of his cornet cut through the moonlit night as his music floated between the clouds and the rippling river.

Of all the music he played, Louis loved the blues and swing best. Together those two forms became the jazz he developed. When Louis heard the blues, the music crawled into his heart and slept inside his soul. He felt the sorrow, the heartbreak of the guy who wrote it. And swing fit his personality, always "up," always ready to see the sunny side of life, always ready to help someone who couldn't see it. Louis liked making people feel better. He was one mellow cat.

CHAPTER 10

Where I Go, You Go

One day Joe Oliver, *the* Joe Oliver, Louis' hero, asked Louis to stop by the club and play a few bars of music. The best part was that Louis brought me along—me, his hock-shop horn. I wanted to impress Joe Oliver too.

Joe thought Louis was a natural. He took a real interest in him. Not like the other musicians who were too busy rushing around or had no time to bother with a kid. Joe gave him tips on playing. He even let Louis carry his cornet. In the world of honky-tonk musicians, *that* was one cool honor. You see, Joe Oliver was the main man in New Orleans jazz.

Then Joe Oliver asked Louis to sit in with his combo one night. Louis was as nervous as a fly in a spider's web. He thought every musician in Joe's band was better than he was.

Louis walked to the front of the stage. They had no mics then. Louis tilted his head back and blew a new kind of blues, blowing notes higher than anyone had ever heard, holding them longer than anyone else—notes that moaned, then turned sugar sweet and soared so high they touched the moon. One by one each note turned colors: first blue, then lazy purple, then spinning round like pink molasses and cotton candy, then into swirls of rainbow-colored ribbons. All floated down as soft as velvet, turning in the air, curling into your ears.

Louis blew with such a passion, he swung with such rhythm that his music made you snap your fingers or swing your big, fat momma hips.

More bandleaders started noticing Louis. They liked his style. They thought he was so darn good, they invited him to sit in with their bands. Sitting in was a way to try out—if the bandleader liked you, he might offer you a spot. Before you could sing "Potato Head Blues," Louis was swinging away, trying out each night. When Louis played, he felt he was *home.*

Night after night after night, he

experimented with music. He tested his ideas, wanting to make music no one else tried and no one else heard, trying to find that music he heard in his head. His music flew free and his rhythm was so contagious that every musician, even the cats in Joe Oliver's band, wanted to

follow his style. It was as if I was part of Louis 'n' he was part of me. My sound was his voice. I, me, the horn, was Louis. Sound crazy? No, that's why we weren't just buddies. We were brothers.

His music set everyone in a fever. And Joe Oliver's ears grew as large as an elephant's as he listened to Louis play his cornet.

It wasn't long before Joe Oliver said, "You're in, Louis. I'll give you a dollar a night."

Louis was so excited! He didn't sleep for the next thirty nights. Mayann still needed money, so Louis continued shoveling coal all day for the Andrews Coal Company. In spite of aching muscles, he played his music every night, all night. Nothing was going to keep him from Joe Oliver's band.

Louis was the best cornet player in the band. He was so good, Joe and Louis started playing duets. They'd get up to the front of the stage and take turns playing solos. It was as if the horns were talking to each other, telling secrets, laughing and teasing, chasing one another around corners. But they mostly played together. Joe Oliver would take the lead and Louis would follow with clever harmony underneath Joe's melody. What Louis did was not an easy-breezy thing to do. He had to be good, yet he couldn't suddenly burst out in a wild melody, strutting his stuff, because Oliver was the leader of the band and the lead horn player.

About that time, Chicago, the jazz center of the world, offered Joe Oliver a job at the famous Lincoln Gardens. It was what Joe Oliver dreamed of. He had to go, but he was worried about leaving Louis. He knew Louis never wanted to leave New Orleans. Louis always told Joe that the New Orleans mud was in his shoes.

One night Joe invited Louis home for supper.

Of course they talked only about music. But Joe also tried to make Louis see that it was important to move forward, not only in music but also to other parts of the country. Joe told Louis, "You gotta grow. You can't stay in the same place playin' the same music. I know you love tryin' new ideas. You belong in Chicago."

Louis didn't want to lose Joe. He was family to Louis—really, more like a father than anyone else had been.

Louis listened, but he didn't say

anything about being willing to move to Chicago or any other place.

Then Joe did something that made Little Louis cry.

"Louis," he said, "your talent is so special that every musician wants to imitate your style. There's no one like you. Your horn's full of miracles. So, I'm givin' you a present. It's *my cornet*. It's time I bought me a new one. Now, take my cornet, little brother."

Louis hugged his hero and his eyes grew watery. Then Louis did something that surprised me and Joe.

Louis kissed *me*, the old hock-shop horn, and said, "No one was more reliable, more dependable than you. You helped me play my kind of music. You're part of me. So I can't leave you. When I'm out on the stage playin' Joe's horn, you'll be waitin' for me in my dressin' room. *Where I go, you go."*

. . .

And that's how Louis rose to fame and I went with him. It wasn't long before Joe Oliver, now called King Oliver, left for Chicago. And it wasn't long after that when he called Louis from Chicago and said, "C'mon up. I need you here."

Louis, who had never left New Orleans, was nervous about going so far. He didn't count the riverboats 'cause they were a short distance away. But when Joe Oliver called, Louis *had* to go.

He heard Chicago was c-c-cold, with a big wind blowing in from the huge lake and the wide sky over Lake Michigan, so Louis bought the longest, warmest under-wear he could find. Then, with a trout sandwich wrapped in a brown paper bag, his underwear folded in another one, and Joe Oliver's cornet under his arm, he boarded the train for Chicago, the Windy City. Of course, I was there too.

Wow! Was he a success. He performed for overflowing crowds, playing his heart out. Every city, every country, every continent wanted him. He was like an eagle soaring toward the sky, into the height of fame. He never slowed down and never stopped playing.

That's the story, the true story of how Louis Armstrong, the great Satchmo, became the world's greatest horn player. Jazz poured from his soul like a river. He loved sharing the music that haunted his heart, that bounced around in his head. When he picked me up to play a solo, I was so proud I felt there wasn't a cornet

around as happy as I was. And there wasn't a horn player as happy as Louis.

He sure loved his music, and he loved the world. And the wonderful thing was, the world loved him back.

AFTERWORD

Louis Armstrong influenced jazz music and jazz musicians throughout the universe. He was a triple threat: he wrote music and lyrics, he was a unique vocalist, and he played the meanest horn. Music critics on every continent regarded him as the finest cornet player in the world. Later, when he switched to the trumpet, he was regarded as the greatest trumpeter. His gravelly, raspy voice was as rough as sandpaper, but still there was something wonderful about it. Everyone loved listening to him.

His ideas changed jazz. Before Louis, no horn player took the mic and played solo for a long stretch of time. Louis encouraged musicians to stand and play for several minutes, a huge difference both to the horn player and to the listener. Louis felt that playing solo showed not only the beauty of the melody but also the skill of the musician.

Before Louis, musicians did not improvise much. Improvisation is creating another thread of music that blends with the melody—and making it up right there, on the spot. When audiences and musicians heard how exciting and free-wheeling it was to create by playing around with the notes in the melody, it encouraged musicians to experiment even more.

Before Louis, vocalists almost never improvised either. They didn't sing that frequently with jazz groups, and they never scatted along with the band. Louis played a big part in freeing them to sing scat, to release their voices, to sound like instruments.

That's not to say that Louis *invented* scat. It started long before, with African tribes who liked to imitate the sounds of the jungle with their drums. And Louis never planned to sing scat profession-ally. But one day his group, the Hot Five, were recording a song when Louis dropped the sheet of paper with lyrics on it. Since he had to sing *on the very next beat*, he didn't have time to pick up the paper and read the words. So Louis scatted. That was the first time Louis recorded scat. He went home very upset. He was sure the record, *Heebie Jeebies*, was going to be the flop of the century. But it was a huge hit!

Louis was not happy taking a day off. He was on the road entertaining people in different states and different countries over three hundred days a year. This was a difficult schedule to sustain, but Louis never minded the difficulties in traveling because he was doing what he loved most: sharing his music with the public. They called him "Ambassador Satch" because his music brought goodwill and helped international relations. He played for many presidents and heads of foreign state, including the king and queen of Great Britain. His records and performances sold out all over France, Germany, Scandinavia, Japan, and the United States.

One day Louis' wife, Lucille, decided that she and Louis had lived out of suitcases and in hotels long enough. So she decided to surprise Louis and buy a home. She found a small two-story house in a working-class neighborhood in Corona, New York. Since Louis had no children of his own, he encouraged the kids on the street to visit. Whenever he returned from a trip on the road, kids would hang out on his stoop, waiting for him to come out and talk with them.

We know all these details about Louis because he wrote in his journal. Louis wrote of each day's events, his feelings about his friends, even the discussions they had in the local barber shop.

His journal reads as if he were talking to a best friend. For a boy who dropped out of fifth grade, Louis enjoyed writing and revealing his thoughts more than friends or family suspected. He talked to the world through his horn, and in writing two autobiographies he shared his life with the world. He lived to be sixty-nine years old.

Louis' home in New York is now the Louis Armstrong House Museum and is open all year for visitors. It is furnished exactly as Lucille Armstrong decorated it, and you can see Louis' study just as it was when he used it. The museum even celebrates his birthday on July 4 in the garden with a huge birthday cake, a jazz concert, and a Louis Armstrong story. Everyone is welcome—just as Louis would have liked it.

GLOSSARY

* slang or street language

blues: music created by African Americans, sad songs about the troubles many of us go through

*cat: a musician who plays jazz, a person who likes jazz

combo: a small group of usually three or four musicians

*cool: knowing a great deal about a subject like art, music, science, or sports

cornet: a small brass horn with valves, a member of the trumpet family

duet: a song by two vocalists or two musicians

freewheeling: flying in many directions; in music, not following the melody

gullet: throat

harmonize: to blend notes in a way that sounds pleasant to the ear

*hightail: to run quickly

*hock shop: a pawnbroker's shop, where you bring something you own to sell for cash or where you buy a secondhand item

*honky-tonks: dance halls, usually small and very cheap; often called by the owner's name, as in Henry Ponce's place

hustler: a hard worker, someone who is always looking for a way to make money

improvise: to create music as you play it, usually including some notes from the melody

instrumental: a musical number with no singer, where just the instruments are heard

jambalaya: Southern food of rice, tomatoes, and fish

jazz: a kind of music started by African Americans and dominated by the blues and a rhythm known as swing; jazz also includes much improvisation

lyrics: the words to a song

*mellow: agreeable, pleased with the world and with your work

mentor: a wise and trusted teacher who guides and teaches you

mournful: full of sadness, full of grieving

outhouse: an outdoor bathroom with no running water, usually made up of four walls, a ceiling, and a door with a small window

peddle: to sell something as you move from place to place

perfect pitch: the ability to sing or recognize the exact note that is being played

*pitch: the story

*put a lid on: to stop

*rag: to bother

ragtime: 1900s music with an off-beat rhythm

raspy: having a scraping sound, like a coarse file rubbing against wood

razzmatazz: showy or flashy—in a good way

riff: an impressive musical phrase played over and over

ruckus: a lot of noise

scat: sounds that don't make sense; silly words that have the beat of the music

shenanigans: trickery, pranks, mischief

soft shoe: a light dance step

solo: a single person performing alone

tarnished: discolored; used to describe metal whose color has been changed by the air, as when copper turns green

tempo: the speed of a piece of music

trumpet: a brass horn with valves and a mouthpiece you blow into

unique: one of a kind, different

vocalist: a singer

wind instrument: an instrument that produces sound because of the air you blow into it; includes cornets, trumpets, saxophones, clarinets, flutes, piccolos, trombones, tubas, and more

REFERENCES

Armstrong, Louis. *Louis Armstrong in His Own Words*. New York: Oxford University Press, 1999.

Armstrong, Louis. *Satchmo: My Life in New Orleans*. New York: Da Capo Press, 1986.

Bergreen, Laurence. *Louis Armstrong: An Extravagant Life*. New York: Broadway Books, 1997.

Brower, Steven. *Satchmo: The Wonderful World and Art of Louis Armstrong.* New York: Abrams, 2009.

Cogswell, Michael. *Louis Armstrong: The Offstage Story of Satchmo.* Portland, OR: Collectors Press, 2003.

Collier, James Lincoln. *Louis Armstrong: An American Genius.* New York: Oxford University Press, 1983.

Collier, James Lincoln. *Louis Armstrong: An American Success Story.* New York: Macmillan Publishing Co., 1985.

Giddins, Gary. *Satchmo.* New York: Doubleday, 1988.

Jones, Max, and John Chilton. *Louis: The Louis Armstrong Story 1900–1971.* New York: Da Capo Press, 1988.

Louis Armstrong: A Cultural Legacy. Marc Miller, ed. Seattle: University of

Washington Press with Queens Museum of
Art, 1994.

Tanenhaus, Sam. *Louis Armstrong.* Black
Americans of Achievement series. New
York: Chelsea House, 1988.

Louis Armstrong House Museum
34-56 107th Street
Corona, NY 11368
www.louisarmstronghouse.org

Muriel Harris Weinstein is a children's book author and poet whose many awards include the Nassau Review Poetry Award, the Fresh Meadows Poetry Award, the Anna Davidson Rosenberg Award, and the Peninsula Award. She has given poetry workshops for children at many libraries and schools, including the UN International School in New York and the Lincoln Center Library for the Performing Arts. Her picture book, *When Louis Armstrong Taught Me Scat*, was a Junior Library Guild Selection. She lives in Great Neck, New York.

Frank Morrison is a renowned fine artist whose work was featured in *Our Children Can Soar*. He has illustrated many picture books, including Alex Rodriguez's *Out of the Ballpark*, Queen Latifah's *Queen of the Scene*, and Brenda C. Roberts's *Jazzy Miz Mozetta*, for which he won the Coretta Scott King/John Steptoe Award for New Talent. He lives in Georgia.

Looking for more pioneers of change?

You can find plenty in *Our Children Can Soar*.

NAACP IMAGE AWARD WINNER

OUR CHILDREN CAN SOAR

A Celebration of Rosa, Barack, and the Pioneers of Change

Michelle Cook

FOREWORD BY
Marian Wright Edelman

Sometimes a person's achievements are so extraordinary, they shape generations to come. From **George Washington Carver** to **Jackie Robinson**, from **Rosa Parks** to **Barack Obama**, this is the story of a people rising and soaring.